This book belong to:

Purfikly Imperfect

BY: KEDRICK T. LOWERY

ILLUSTRATED BY:
OBAYOMI AANUOLUWAPO AND DIRISU DAVID

Published by Kedrick T. Lowery

Durham, NC

Library of Congress Control Number: 2020917909

Printed in the United States of America

ISBN: 979-8-9896748-3-1

DEDICATION

To every child who has ever felt different, this book is for you. May you always remember that your uniqueness is your strength, and that being purfikly imperfect is what makes you truly special.

With all my love,
Dr. Kedrick T. Lowery

● ● ● ● ●

ACKNOWLEDGEMENT

My sincerest appreciation is extended to Layla Grayce, Laura Nicole, and Dr. Siti Lowery… the Princesses and the Queen of my life. Thank you for all you do and thank you being you.

I am purfikly imperfect
from my head down to my toes
I am purfikly imperfect
from my eyes, to my ears, to my
mouth, and my nose

I used to look in the mirror
and struggle with what I would see
But now I look in the mirror
and appreciate all of me

I appreciate my body
whether big, large, tiny or small
I appreciate my body
whether fat, skinny, short or tall

I am purfikly imperfect in all that
you see
I am imperfectly perfect and I love
all of me

Others see my imperfections
some laugh and some call me names
But when I see my imperfections
I shake off all the shame

I love my hair
whether long, short, kinky, curly or
straight
I love my hair
brown, black, blond or grey

I am purfikly imperfect in all that
you see
I am imperfectly perfect and I love
all of me

Some people dislike others
because of the color of their skin
But I love everyone
because I'm comfortable with the
skin I'm in

I am comfortable with skins that are
lighter
Some olive, some yellow and some
white

I am comfortable with skins that are darker
Some black, some brown all skins tones are just right

I am purfikly imperfect in all that
you see
I am imperfectly perfect and I love
all of me

Being purfik is not possible
because my imperfections others
always see
They don't know being imperfect
is what makes me uniquely me

I am unique when I am up
I am unique when I am down

I am unique when I smile
I am unique when I frown

I am purfikly imperfect in all that
you see
I am imperfectly perfect and I love
all of me

I used to compare myself to others
like them I would try to be
Now I know I am purfikly
imperfect
and I am happy being me

ABOUT THE AUTHOR

Dr. Kedrick T. Lowery is a Life Coach, Speaker, Author, Marriage and Family Counselor, Mentor, Pastor and most importantly a Husband (of Dr. Siti) and Father (of Layla Grayce and Laura Nicole). Lowery brings over 25 years of education and experiences to his passion for living and helping others live their best life.

www.ingramcontent.com/pod-product-compliance
Lightning Source LLC
Chambersburg PA
CBHW041624110726

48005CB00002B/489